Published in Great Britain in 2011 by Shire Publications
Ltd, Midland House, West Way, Botley, Oxford OX2 0PH,
United Kingdom.
44-02 23rd Street, Suite 219, Long Island City, NY 11101,
USA.

E-mail: shire@shirebooks.co.uk   www.shirebooks.co.uk

© 2011 Shire Publications.

A CIP catalogue record for this book is available from the
British Library.

Shire Living Histories no. 9.   ISBN-13: 978 0 74780 829 9

Mike Brown has asserted his right under the Copyright,
Designs and Patents Act, 1988, to be identified as the
author of this book.

Designed by Myriam Bell Design, France and typeset in
Perpetua, Jenson Text and Gill Sans.

Printed in China through Worldprint Ltd.

11 12 13 14 15   10 9 8 7 6 5 4 3 2 1

COVER IMAGE
Father and son, complete with gas masks and helmets,
standing outside their Anderson shelter. Many families had
an 'Anderson' in the back garden; they were damp and
drafty, but they gave some level of protection from the air
raids. (Author's collection)

PHOTOGRAPH ACKNOWLEDGEMENTS

Crown Copyright, pages 4, 6, 10, 11, 14 (top), 16 (left
and right), 17, 30 (left and right), 39, 44 (left), 46, 47
(lower), 48, 52 (upper and lower), 53 (lower), 67, 72
(bottom left and right), 73, 76; Imperial War Museum,
pages 12, 14 (bottom), 20 (bottom), 23, 27, 44 (right),
47 (top), 62, 64 (top and bottom), 68, 75; Lewisham
Local Archives, page 65; Robert Opie Collection, page 18;
ROSPA, page 51. All other illustrations are from the
author's collection.

AUTHOR ACKNOWLEDGEMENTS

I would like to thank the following people who have made
this book possible; my wife Carol and sons Will and Ralph
for their patience and support. Christa Hook for some
brilliant artwork. I must especially thank my editor
Ruth Sheppard, who has made the project such a joy to
work on.

IMPERIAL WAR MUSEUMS COLLECTIONS

Some of the photos in this book come from the Imperial
War Museum's huge collections which cover all aspects of
conflict involving Britain and the Commonwealth since the
start of the twentieth century. These rich resources are
available online to search, browse and buy at
www.iwmcollections.org.uk. In addition to Collections
Online, you can visit the Visitor Rooms where you can
explore over 8 million photographs, thousands of hours of
moving images, the largest sound archive of its kind in the
world, thousands of diaries and letters written by people
in wartime, and a huge reference library. To make an
appointment, call (020) 7416 5320, or e-mail
mail@iwm.org.uk. Imperial War Museum
www.iwm.org.uk

Shire Publications is supporting the Woodland Trust, the UK's leading woodland conservation charity, by funding the dedication of trees.

Staffordshire Library and Information Service
Please return or renew or by the last date shown

W

If not required by other readers, this item may be renewed
in person, by post or telephone, online or by email.
To renew, either the book or ticket are required

**24 Hour Renewal Line
0845 33 00 740**

Staffordshire
County Council

SHIRE LIVING HISTORIES

How we worked • How we played • How we lived

CONTENTS

COMBINED

OPERATIONS

INCLUDE YOU

PRINTED FOR H.M. STATIONERY OFFICE BY CHROMOWORKS LTD. LONDON. 51-4292.

ISSUED BY THE ADMIRALTY.

PREFACE

'LET US brace ourselves to our duties, and so bear ourselves, that if the British Empire and its Commonwealth last for a thousand years, men will still say, "this was their finest hour".' Even in June 1940, little over a month after becoming prime minister and with more than five years of struggle still to come, Winston Churchill fully understood the enormity of the challenge, and the greatness of the response that Britons would make to the threat of, first Nazism and Fascism in Europe, and later aggressive imperialism in East Asia. Every man, woman and child in the country was asked to commit themselves, in great ways and in small, and the vast majority responded heroically. Evacuation, dried eggs, blackouts, air-raid shelters, *ITMA*: the humdrum reality of life on the home front has become as much part of our folk memories about the war as the terrifying conflict in the air and at sea, and the great set-piece battles fought on three continents. The younger generations sometimes find it hard to comprehend that all this, so different from our present way of life, lies within the living memory of their grandparents and great-grandparents, forming their outlook for the rest of their lives.

Mike Brown offers a brisk survey of the preparations for the looming conflict in the 1930s, before exploring the realities of life in wartime Britain. With fascinating details and lively illustrations, he shows how life went on and Britons 'came through', even in the most difficult of circumstances. Avoiding the nostalgia and rose-tinted spectacles that sometimes distort our image of these years, he shows how the authorities organised health, education, food and fuel supplies and much else to ensure, so far as possible, fairness for all.

Peter Furtado
General Editor

Opposite: Factory work poster. Not everyone could fight but, as this poster shows, everyone could do their bit for the war effort.

5

SERVE TO SAVE

BRITAIN PREPARES FOR WAR

THE 1930S WERE A TURBULENT DECADE in Europe, when the new ideologies of communism, socialism and fascism led to street fighting, civil war in Spain, and fascist governments in first Italy, then Germany. Britain also had its share of such troubles, culminating in the 'Battle of Cable Street' when Oswald Mosley's British Union of Fascists, otherwise known as the Blackshirts, attempted to march through London's East End in October 1936. They were opposed by anti-fascists, including Jews, socialists and communists and the march turned into a vicious, running street battle.

The British government was determined to stay out of European entanglements, fearing that Britain would be drawn into a war as in 1914, yet in September 1938 it found itself on the verge of just such a crisis.

Czechoslovakia, created by the Versailles Treaty of 1919 from pieces of the Austro-Hungarian empire, had a multi-ethnic population, of whom a quarter were German speakers from the Sudetenland; this had never been part of Germany, but after the takeover of Austria Hitler demanded it. This posed a problem, as France was committed by treaty to support Czechoslovakia in the event of German aggression, and Britain was committed to support France. Prime Minister Neville Chamberlain summed up the feelings of many when he described the crisis as 'a quarrel in a far-away country between people of whom we know nothing.'

Neither Germany nor Czechoslovakia would give way, and war looked inevitable. In Britain, hasty preparations were made: in expectation of mass air raids, trenches were dug in parks and open land; people in designated danger areas, mainly the larger towns and cities, were issued with gas masks; and the authorities prepared for the evacuation of two million people from London.

Opposite: Early ARP recruitment poster, showing a man protecting a woman and child. Soon the focus would shift, and such posters would appeal to women to volunteer.

Below: German postcard celebrating the Anschluss of 1938. In the process of appeasement, Britain and France stood by while Nazi Germany expanded.

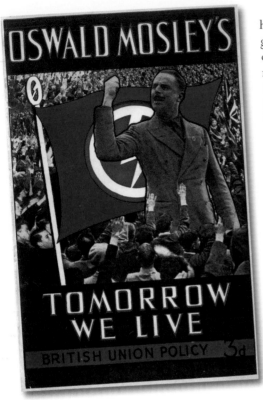

Cover of Oswald Mosley's book, *Tomorrow We Live*. The British Union of Fascists was a potent right-wing force in the 1930s, when such groups were active throughout Europe.

Included in those to be evacuated were half a million schoolchildren who would go in school groups, and in the last few days of September, anxious parents received letters such as that sent from Brockley Central School, dated 27 September, which began: 'Dear parents, will you have your boy's luggage ready Wednesday morning. If you live more than fifteen minutes walk from the school, he must bring his case with him on Wednesday morning.' They would have been even more anxious had they known that there were absolutely no arrangements made for housing or feeding the children when they arrived at their (undisclosed) destinations. Luckily, in the event, this planned evacuation was called off before the vast majority of the children went.

A last-minute meeting was held in Munich between Hitler, Chamberlain, Daladier of France, and Mussolini. There was little debate; Chamberlain and Daladier meekly gave in, handing Hitler everything he wanted. The Czechs were not even in the meeting, being presented with a fait accompli by the British and French, and told that if they did not accept the agreement, they would be left to fight the German army alone.

The news was greeted with wild excitement in Britain and France; André Maurois wrote: 'American Public Opinion was severely critical of Chamberlain and Daladier... They had little idea of the state of mind of the Citizens of Paris and London who saw themselves without air-raid shelters, without gas masks and without anti-aircraft guns, while there circulated, thanks to the efficiency of German propaganda, terrifying rumours about two-ton bombs the very breath of which could destroy whole sections of a City and about poison gasses that would be released from above them.'

Poison gas was the terror weapon of the decade. Stories of its use in the First World War, and photographs and paintings of gas casualties all added to the fear of bombing amongst the public, as did cinema newsreel films of bombing in Spain, Abyssinia and China.

The euphoria of Munich was short-lived and for many Chamberlain's boast of 'peace for our time' rang hollow. A mass-observation report from Barrow-in-Furness, noted that 'Quite half seem to think we are "putting off war" till we are in a stronger position. There was not the joyful feeling abroad I had expected. It was there certainly but the prevailing spirit was of wariness if not doubt. And resentment that we had to "give in" to Hitler.'

Civil defence preparations had begun some time before Munich; in February 1938 'black-out' plans were announced, banning all exterior lighting from shops, homes and motor vehicles in time of war, while an air raid warning system was already well-established by the time of the Munich crisis. These official plans needed people on the ground to carry them out; wardens, rescue squads, first aid workers, yet there was a very poor response to appeals for volunteers. Munich saw Britain's Air Raid Precautions (ARP) services woefully short of trained personnel, but the crisis changed all that, with a surge of people coming forward to train during and immediately after it.

THE PILGRIM OF PEACE
BRAVO! MR. CHAMBERLAIN

Above: Postcard from the period of the Munich agreement, October 1938. For a short period, Neville Chamberlain was seen as a hero, but the mood soon changed.

AIR RAID PROTECTION

SECURITY

IS THE BEST INSURANCE
IS ONLY EFFECTIVE IF COMPLETE
IS ONLY PRACTICABLE IF THE COST IS LOW

Rooms in the Average House cannot be made to give
COMPLETE PROTECTION AT REASONABLE COST.

THE "EFFECTIVE"
AIR RAID SHELTER
GIVES COMPLETE SECURITY AT LOW COST

IT IS . . .
Splinter and Blast Proof.
Gas Proof.
Independent of Public Services.
Proof against Overcrowding.
Watertight.
Complete in all essentials.
Always Ready for use.

IT HAS . . .
A Filtered Air Supply.
Sanitary Accommodation.
Alternative Exits.
Easily-lifted Trapdoors.
It will require no maintenance.
It is always ready for use.

Regd. Design No. 827,359. Prov. Patent No. 16,410, dated 1.6.38

THE COST as shown above. Designed for seven persons, including Emergency Exit, Air-Conditioning Plant and Lavatory. Materials only £70. Cost, complete and erected (according to site conditions), approximately £90. Variations reducing the cost are possible. Send for detailed particulars of this and other types to . . .

BRACEY & CLARK LTD.
100 CECIL ST., WATFORD, HERTS.
'PHONE: WATFORD 4888

Left: Advertisement for a private air raid shelter from 1938. The government encouraged householders to provide their own shelter as part of its dispersal policy.

9

Right: First of a series of Civil Defence pamphlets delivered to every house in Britain in the summer of 1939, giving the householders details of how to prepare themselves and their house for the event of war.

Far right: Humorous postcard on the blackout. In spite of its message, there was a great deal of grumbling about the blackout during the 'phoney war' period of 1939/40. With the coming of the Blitz, all that changed.

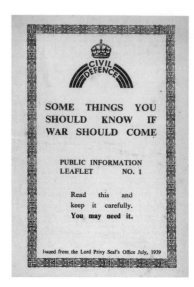

LETS BE CHEERFUL IN THE GLOOM

WHEN YOU'RE FEELING OUT OF HUMOUR,
IF YOU HEAR A STARTLING RUMOUR,
KEEP IT DARK!
SHROUD YOUR HOUSE & DO NOT GRUMBLE,
THO' IN PITCH-BLACK STREETS YOU STUMBLE,
KEEP THEM DARK! Roz

Householders were encouraged to prepare for raids, with advice issued on building trenches in the back garden, making a room into a gas-proof refuge room, or installing a shelter. Building firms advertised private shelters supplied and erected in your garden. The take up before October 1938 was disappointing, but once again Munich changed all that – suddenly there was a flurry of activity.

A month after Munich Sir John Anderson was put in charge of ARP. He promised a mass-produced shelter which people could erect themselves in their own homes, supplied free to poorer families. This would become the famous 'Anderson' shelter.

In mid-March 1939, in spite of Hitler's promises at Munich, German troops marched into what was left of Czechoslovakia. All eyes looked to Hitler's next target – the Polish city of Danzig. At the end of March Chamberlain guaranteed Polish independence. True to form, Hitler now began to demand that Danzig be handed over to Germany. Preparations for war were scaled up; once again schools prepared for evacuation, and on a far greater scale than London alone, and the problems encountered at the time of Munich were borne in mind.

In July 1939, every household in Britain received a set of official Civil Defence pamphlets through the post; the first was entitled 'Some Things You Should Know If War Should Come', which began 'The object of this leaflet is to tell you now some of the things you ought to know if you are to be ready for the emergency of war. This does not mean that war is expected now, but it is everyone's duty to be prepared for the possibility of war.' The pamphlet went on to outline the main schemes being prepared by the authorities. Subsequent pamphlets looked in more depth at gas masks, and masking windows – later to be universally known as 'the blackout'; evacuation, food in wartime, and fire precautions.

On the blackout, 'the most convenient way of shutting in the light is to use close fitting blinds. These can be of any thick, dark coloured material such as dark blue or black or dark green glazed Holland, Lancaster or Italian Cloth. If you cannot manage this, you could obscure your windows by fixing up sheets of black paper or thick dark brown paper mounted on battens … Make sure that no light shows when your front door or back door is open. In some cases it may be possible to fix a curtain in the hall or passage to form a light lock, but if this cannot be done, the light must be turned off before the door is opened.'

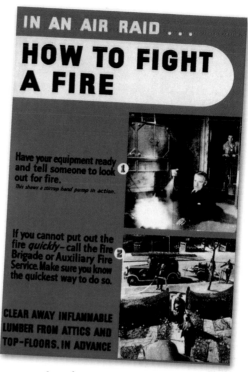

'Do not leave things until the last, but get together the materials which you think you would need. If you wait, you might find that you have difficulty in getting what you wanted.'

On the subject of fire precautions, it was pointed out that, in an air raid, fire bombs might well be used, in which case the local fire brigade would be unable to cope with all the fires started 'unless the householder himself and his family took the first steps in defending their home.' These small fire bombs would punch through the roof of a building, often ending up in the loft space where they would start a blaze. To this end the instructions were, once again, not to wait for the outbreak of a war, but to immediately clear your roof spaces and attics of any junk, and to make sure that you could easily get into the roof space. You should also have ready 'at least four large buckets, a shovel or scoop, preferably with a long handle, and a fair quantity of sand or dry earth' and if possible, a stirrup hand pump, or failing this, 'a garden syringe would be useful, or even old blankets soaked in water.'

Throughout the summer preparations accelerated, as did attempts at negotiation, but when German troops marched into Poland on 1 September 1939, war was inevitable.

Government poster showing how to deal with incendiary bombs. Notice the trailer pump in the lower photograph being towed by a saloon car, with a white line painted around its edge for the blackout.

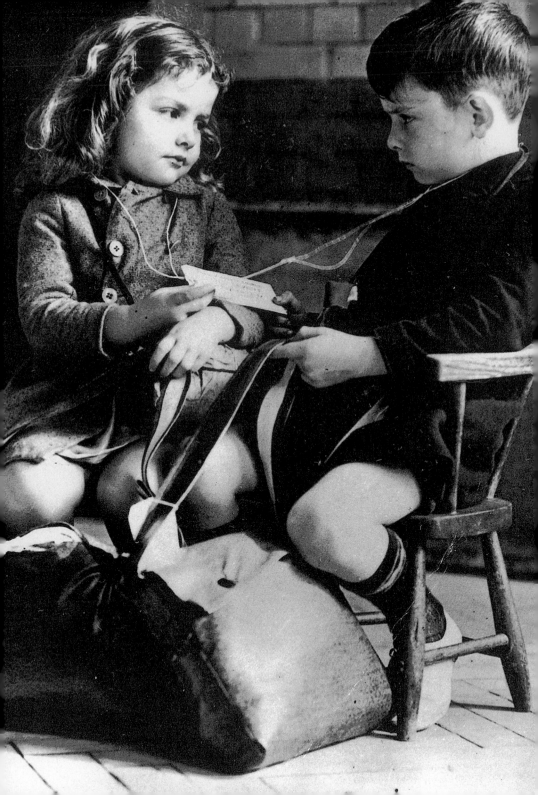

Family Life

A S WAR BROKE OUT, plans were put into operation that would change the lives of British families. Many young men left for the forces. In mid-1939 the regular army numbered 224,000, supplemented by 320,000 members of the Territorial Army. Further recruiting took place during the summer, and to this number were added 150,000 men of the reserve, called up on the outbreak of war, bringing the British army up to a total of 865,000 by the first week of the war. There were also young women, but they were far fewer in number – in September 1939 there were a total of 17,000 women in the women's auxiliary services.

A far greater number of children were also on the move; the haphazard evacuation plans at the time of Munich had been much improved. The plan now covered evacuation from cities and towns from Portsmouth to Dundee, while possible billets had been surveyed in safe areas and recorded by the Women's Voluntary Services (WVS).

Children from the 'evacuation areas' were to be evacuated with their schools, and billeted with householders in the 'reception areas', while children from handicapped, special and nursery schools would be housed together in places such as stately homes. Mothers of children under the age of five could accompany their children, and take any older siblings with them.

Throughout the earlier part of 1939, rehearsals had taken place; parents had received lists of clothes, food, washing things, books, card games, and of course, their child's gas mask, to have ready, and teachers, who would be accompanying their classes, had prepared for the move. On 24 August – during the summer holiday – the BBC broadcast a notice to teachers of schools that were to be evacuated, summoning them back to their schools. On 1 September the order to start evacuation was given.

Of the five-and-a-half million who qualified for the government evacuation scheme, only about a third actually went, but this still

Opposite: Two young evacuees, with their labels, on their way into the unknown. Evacuation was often a traumatic experience. (IWM HU 36217)

LEAVE THIS TO US
SONNY — <u>YOU</u> OUGHT
TO BE OUT OF LONDON

MINISTRY OF HEALTH EVACUATION SCHEME

Evacuation was not compulsory, and the government worked hard to convince parents to send their children away from the danger areas with posters such as this one.

Militiamen called up 'for the emergency' in 1939 receive their kit. These would be the first of millions of young men and women called up to the armed forces over the next few years. (IWM 28/8A)

meant that over a million schoolchildren, and three-quarters of a million young children and mothers were on the move that September, by bus, coach, train and river steamer.

Families were therefore split up, by fathers and older sons called up to the forces – later to be joined by their sisters joining the women's auxiliary forces – and by younger siblings evacuated from the danger areas. Some married men found themselves living in an empty house as their wife and young children moved away to safety.

In the reception areas, families were changed by additions: evacuees billeted with them were not always welcome additions, as, whilst evacuation was voluntary, billeting was not. Problems were particularly encountered where the mothers of young children were billeted, and many of them returned home. Other problems included communication (at a time when local accents were less widely familiar), religion, and the differences in regional diets, but in most cases billeters and evacuees settled down together 'for the duration'.

"THINKIN' OH! MY DARLING LOVE OF THEE!"
(WITH APOLOGIES TO CYRIL FLETCHER.)

Many mothers with young children were evacuated with them, leaving 'Dad' to cope on his own, as is shown in this humorous postcard.

Evacuation would ebb and flow, following the events of the war. As the 'phoney war' dragged on and the threatened bombing failed to materialise, many returned home. Then with the blitzkrieg on the Continent in the spring of 1940, a fresh wave of evacuation took place, added to by the fall of France. As Britain then prepared for invasion, with the south and east coasts likely landing grounds, qualifying residents, as well as evacuees who had been billeted there, were moved to the west. Fresh waves joined them with the start in earnest of the bombing Blitz in September, and then once again in 1944 with the commencement of the V-weapon attacks.

There was also a lot of 'private evacuation', where people who didn't qualify for the government scheme left the danger areas, or those who did qualify were sent to relatives in the country. It was estimated that as many as two million people took part in private evacuation between June and September 1939. Some of these were what were called 'bomb dodgers', and for them the property pages of papers advertised houses or cottages to buy or rent 'in a quiet area', or 'in a peaceful setting', while hotels and boarding houses used similar phrases to attract those wary of the threatened bombing.

House adverts from the *Daily Express*, 2 September 1939. 'Safer zones', 'safety areas', etc, were thinly veiled references to areas less likely to be bombed.

Above: As more and more men were needed by the armed forces, women were increasingly needed to take their places in the factories.

Above right: With their menfolk away fighting, women were required to do all those jobs traditionally seen as 'men's work'. The government tried to help out with leaflets such as this one.

In 1939, the number of unemployed stood at about a million; this quickly fell to a little over 100,000. In late May 1940 a report spelled out a shortfall: one-and-a-half million workers would have to be found if Britain were to maintain production. This could only be done by bringing new workers into play, and in the main this meant using women. Official schemes encouraged women to volunteer, but these attracted hundreds of responses rather than the thousands the government needed. The authorities began moving towards a wider conscription, first by 'freezing' volunteer posts, such as in civil defence, meaning that volunteers could no longer resign. Eventually, in late 1941, there was no alternative; the conscription of women had to be introduced.

In order to release mothers for war work, school dinners were provided for children, as were nurseries for children under five; but for older children the streets and the bomb sites became playgrounds. With fathers absent, and mothers at work or returning home tired, children were often left to their own devices. Juvenile delinquency became a real problem, fuelled by the black market, with its underlying petty theft and easy money.

It was not only in industry that women took over from the men – in households up and down the country, wives had to run the house in the absence of husbands serving in the forces, and this meant moving into traditionally male preserves such as changing fuses, fitting plugs, minor (and sometimes major) repairs, decorating, and dealing with finances. As ever, the women's magazines came to their aid with articles and tips.

Gardening, especially the more heavy-duty side of gardening such as vegetable growing, had long been seen as a male preserve. It was known from the experience of the First World War that one of Britain's weaknesses was that most of the nation's food was imported. As in the First World War, German U-boats and surface raiders would try to starve the country into submission by sinking the ships bringing in food. Growing as much food as possible, soon known as 'digging for victory', would be a vital part of the

war effort. Men, women and children could all help, cultivating food in their gardens and on allotments. Newspapers, magazines and the radio were full of advice, with the 'Radio Gardener', Cecil Middleton, known universally as Mr Middleton, becoming something of a national treasure.

Another area that every member of the family could help with was salvage. Britain did not only rely on imported food, but other natural resources as well. To try to lessen this, salvage, what we would now call recycling, was vital. The nation was kept at the task by paper drives, collecting aluminium saucepans for aircraft manufacture, iron gates and railings for munitions, and rubber, rags and bones.

In 1945, with the demobilisation of the members of the armed forces, and the return of the evacuees, families began to get back together. However, there were a significant number of families who would never be together again. Over 60,000 civilians and 380,000 members of the services had died; some evacuees never returned, and a few parents refused to have them back; while there were 38,000 divorces in 1945, as almost six years of separation had its effect.

Raw materials had to be conserved, and this meant salvage. All sorts of waste – paper, glass, rubber, bones, metal – was recycled.

When the AIR RAID warning goes—
What shall we DO?

Issued by the A.R.P. Committee of
SOUTHAMPTON
For the Protection of yourself and your family.

HOME AND
NEIGHBOURHOOD

IN THE INTER-WAR YEARS poison gas took a hold on the public mind as an ever-present nightmare threat which coloured international relations, in the same way that nuclear weapons would in the sixties. In 1934 the British government decided to build up a stock of gas masks to be issued to the public in an emergency, and production began in 1936.

Three types were needed: a mask for civilians from the age of four upwards, a mask for children from about eighteen months to four years old, and a baby's respirator. Unlike the other two the babies' version was not a mask, as it covered virtually the whole baby, hence its nickname: the 'baby bag'.

Respirators were first issued to people living in danger areas at the time of the Munich crisis. Distribution to all those who had not received them began again in the summer of 1939, and by the time war broke out, the issue of the general mask was virtually complete: but children's masks and babies' respirators were still in worryingly short supply. Their issue would not be complete until late October in the case of baby bags, and the end of January 1940 for children's masks.

There was no legal obligation for people to carry their mask, and from the start not everyone did. For those who did so the cardboard box in which they were issued doubled, with the addition of a length of string, as a carrying case. Many preferred to buy a cloth, leather or metal case, and many private companies did a thriving trade in these. By Christmas 1939, the non-appearance of the feared air raids, or the use of gas on the battlefields, meant that the vast majority ceased to carry their masks.

Another anti-gas measure was the refuge room. Householders were advised to put one room aside as a gas-proof room, for use by the family in the event of a poison gas attack. Windows, floorboards and fireplaces had to be sealed with tape, and an airlock created in

Opposite:
There was a great deal of advice published about what to do in an air raid, such as this booklet from Southampton. As with all advice, some of it was very useful, some obvious, and some downright confusing.

How to put on a
civilian gas mask,
as shown on a
cigarette card
from 1938. The
civilian gas mask
was issued to
everyone above
the age of
about five.

This rather
sinister
photograph
shows a nurse
and baby wearing
gas masks. The
gas helmet for
infants, or 'baby
bag', enclosed the
baby's head and
entire torso.
(IWM D 648)

20

the doorway by hanging an old carpet over it. Lists were published of items to have in your refuge room such as food, water and a first aid kit, things to pass the time such as books, games and so on, and provisions for more fundamental needs, such as a chamber pot or bucket, toilet paper etc. In the event few people actually had the space, time or inclination to create such a room.

There had a been a rash of private air raid shelters built during and after the Munich crisis, but the government were aware that many families could not afford such shelters. The authorities, sticking with the idea of sheltering at home, decided to issue a cheap, mass-produced shelter which people could erect themselves in their own garden, free to those with an income of not more than £250 a year, and to this end the Anderson shelter was developed.

Made from corrugated iron sheets, it was bolted together inside a hole in the garden. This meant that it could easily be adapted for larger families by the addition of more corrugated sheets. The first were delivered in February 1939 to householders in Islington. By April nearly 300,000 had been delivered, and on the outbreak of the war, almost one-and-a-half million Andersons were in use.

For those who did not qualify for a free shelter, Andersons could be bought, although at first delivery was limited to those entitled to free distribution. One month after war broke out they went on sale, costing between £6 14s and £10 18s, depending on size. In the meantime, those without either an Anderson or a private shelter relied on digging a trench, or dugout, in the back garden. Many men were

Comic postcard of an Anderson shelter. They were most certainly not built for comfort. Cramped, drafty, and often flooded, they did, however, offer some protection.

ex-soldiers, for whom this was second nature, but for others the authorities issued plans for building such shelters.

For those who had no garden, and for people caught outside, there were public shelters. Some were specially built brick shelters, while in other places caves, the basements of public and commercial buildings, and tunnels were utilised, as had happened during the First World War.

Although there were no actual raids for some time, there were several warnings, and people spent many hours in their shelters. As these became a regular event, people turned them into something of a social event, by sharing shelters with friends or neighbours, taking it in turns to visit each other's shelters. People tried to make the best of their time under warning by installing battery radios and wind-up gramophones in their shelters, and taking board games, cards and books with them.

The Blitz began in earnest in September 1940, and as it continued into the winter the chief drawbacks of the Anderson – its propensity to flooding and drafts – became a real problem, especially as people began to spend whole nights in the shelter.

A garden dugout, as shown on a cigarette card. The dugout was a sort of glorified trench for those who did not have an air raid shelter. For many veterans of the First World War, building these was second nature.

Many moved to the public shelters in spite of shared communal toilets, shelter cough and crowding, or just stayed indoors, in order to get a decent night's sleep.

By now the government had seen the need for an indoor shelter. The answer was the Morrison, or table shelter, available from early 1941. This was described as resembling 'a large dining-room table of stout steel. Underneath are springs to support a mattress, and walls of steel netting are fitted to prevent injury from flying debris.' When not in use as a shelter it could be used as a table by removing the side netting panels. It became common for the children of the family to sleep in the Morrison, and be joined by their parents in the event of a raid. As with the Anderson they were available free to those on low income, or alternatively could be bought for £7.

Elsewhere around the home, there were other air raid precautions to be taken. Chief amongst them was the blackout; all windows and doors had to be made light-proof during the hours of blackout – usually half an hour after sunset until half an hour before sunrise, the times were printed on the front of newspapers. If blinds were used they had to be of stout material and dark in colour, covering the window completely; curtains had to be dark and thick. If they had no thick curtains, people used blankets, pieces of carpet, lino, or even thick sheets of brown paper to cover windows. Doors to the outside had to be screened, often by a blanket or curtain

Overleaf:
Typical scene in a wartime suburban living room c. 1941. The table is cleared after the evening meal and dad, in Home Guard uniform, is just leaving for duty. The kids are playing cards on the Morrison table shelter, while mum is carrying out that most common of wartime tasks – knitting. In the background the windows have been taped to prevent flying splinters of glass caused by blast, while in the foreground the wireless is providing the evening's entertainment. (Artwork by Christa Hook)

A Morrison or table shelter. These were erected inside the house, and when not in use, could also do duty as a table. (IWM D 2055)

hung inside, so that no light could be seen when the door was opened. Failure to comply with the blackout would result in a stiff reprimand from the local Air Raid Wardens – 'Put that light out!' – and repeated transgressions could result in court action and a heavy fine.

Windows were also the subject of blast-protection in the form of netting stuck over them, or covered criss-cross with sticky tape (far less effective and not officially advised), to decrease the chances of injury by flying pieces of glass.

Incendiary bombs could cause havoc in urban areas, completely overwhelming the fire services who had to prioritise hospitals, factories and other critical facilities, leaving householders to deal with incendiaries themselves. For this there were many devices, from the simple bag or bucket of sand or earth, to scoops, pumps and extinguishers. The most effective extinguisher was the stirrup pump, developed for the purpose. Neighbours often clubbed together to buy one, and displayed a sign in windows or on gates stating 'stirrup pump here'. Groups of neighbours were encouraged to form themselves

Incendiary bombs, whilst small, could start major fires. Householders were encouraged to tackle incendiaries themselves, such as by pouring sand on them with a long-handled scoop.

CHURCHMAN'S CIGARETTES

CONTROL OF INCENDIARY BOMB

into 'street fire parties', organising rotas to take it in turns to act as neighbourhood fire watchers, calling out their teams should incendiaries be dropped, to extinguish them before the fire became serious. In 1941 these teams were formalised with the creation of the 'fire guard', into which everyone not involved in other war service had to be enrolled.

Even the church was affected by war. The blackout was a particular nightmare for churches, with their massive stained-glass windows, and 1940 saw the banning of the ringing of church bells — bell-ringing was only to be used as a signal of invasion, bringing out the Home Guard, originally the Local Defence Volunteers. These were part-time soldiers who would serve as local anti-invasion troops. Many Home Guardsmen were too old for conscription, often old soldiers. This, and the fact that at first they had no uniforms and few weapons, made them a bit of a joke, and led to their common name: 'Dad's Army'. In spite of the restrictions put in place, the church became a centre for social work, local celebration, and war-related fund-raising.

A typical member of the Home Guard. Their average age being well over the age of conscription, they gained the nickname 'Dad's Army', but most of them were veterans of the trenches in the First World War, and not to be laughed at. (IWM D 6795)

WORK

IN SEPTEMBER 1939, Britain's existing armed forces were clearly not big enough to win the war, and further expansion was necessary. There was a rush to join up but many were disappointed to find that the authorities had no intention of being swamped by untrained recruits. The armed forces would be expanded in an orderly, if somewhat slow manner – volunteers were told to go home and await their call-up.

For some this was not quick enough and they turned to other war jobs, the ARP or the auxiliary fire brigade. Others were in what were called reserved occupations – jobs regarded as vital to the nation. This not only meant that you couldn't be called up – you could not even join up if you wanted to. Some jobs were completely reserved, such as lighthouse keepers or medical students, while others had age limitations: thirty in the case of railway porters, twenty-three for motor mechanics, and so on. Some could join the forces in their trade capacity, such as doctors. In 1941 the idea of reserved occupations was scrapped; block reservations of particular jobs were replaced by the reservation of key individual workers.

A few months before war broke out an act was introduced under which men between the ages of twenty and twenty-one had to register for six months' military training. In October 1939 it was announced that all men aged eighteen to forty-one, not in reserved occupations, could be called up to the armed services.

Conscription was done in batches; men of a certain age were split up into groups, and called up in turn to undertake basic training before being posted into different units. That October the first groups of men aged between twenty and twenty-three were called up.

Those who, for moral or religious reasons, felt unable to take part in a war were known as conscientious objectors. They had to apply to a panel of officials who could grant them full exemption from any kind of war work, from military service only, or dismiss their claim

Opposite:
A roof spotter. His job was to raise the alarm if he saw German aircraft approaching. Relying on spotters instead of acting on every air raid warning siren reduced disruption of production.

where's yours?

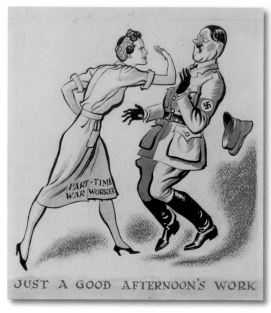

PART-TIME WAR WORKER

JUST A GOOD AFTERNOON'S WORK

Above: ARP recruiting poster. The Air Raid Precautions services needed thousands of volunteers to train as wardens, rescue workers and in the casualty services.

Above right: War work poster. As the war went on and more men were needed for the forces, so women were desperately needed to keep the factories going.

altogether. Of the 60,000 applications, almost a third were dismissed. Many of those whose cases were upheld went on to work on farms, as ambulance drivers, stretcher-bearers, or in bomb-disposal units.

On 18 December 1941, a parliamentary act was brought in making all adults – men and women – liable for national service. At first, only single women between the ages of twenty and thirty were called up and they were allowed to opt to go either into the forces or into industry; as with men, some women claimed conscientious objector status. Within a couple of months, all women between eighteen and sixty had to register with the Ministry of Labour, whether married or single, with or without children. By mid-1943, nearly eight million women were in employment, including almost ninety per cent of single women, and three million married and widowed women. Against a great deal of resistance, and much grumbling, women virtually took over the factory floor in many places, and found, sometimes to their own, and often much to their male co-workers' surprise, that they could do the job well.

As the war went on more and more people were needed for the war effort; the armed forces would need to be increased by over three million (by 1941 there were three-and-a-quarter million in the armed forces including over 200,000 women in the auxiliary forces, rising steadily to four-and-a-half million in 1944 including 350,000 women). At the same time the numbers required to support the forces increased, with those working in munitions and other war-related industries such as shipbuilding increasing from two-and-a-half million to three-and-a-quarter million. By 1941 there were also over 350,000 full-time workers in civil defence.

Both those conscripted to the armed forces or into industry were put through a medical test, then sent for a period of training. This was well-depicted in several wartime films; *The Way Ahead* (1944), for instance, shows a motley band of militiamen (as conscripts were called) going through their training, while *Millions Like Us* (1943) looked at the lives of conscripted women in an armaments factory.

The influx of women was not the only change facing British industry. The demands of war meant that production methods had to be radically improved. Aircraft production was of particular concern, and a Ministry of Aircraft Production was set up in May 1940. During that crucial summer, with the threat of invasion hovering and the Battle of Britain going on overhead, war-related factories began working twenty-four hours a day, seven days a week; with many working twelve-hour shifts. Workers often slept at their factories, especially when the Blitz began and air raids made travel in the evenings difficult.

A typical group of female factory workers wearing a range of overalls and boilersuits. Note also the hairstyles, glasses and make-up.

The workforce in a typical factory was made up of both men and women, increasingly women, the men either in a reserved status because of their skills or too old or unfit for active service. There were advantages to factory work: pay was good – better than the national average, and those lucky enough to find themselves in a parachute factory could keep the silk offcuts to make items such as underwear or blouses.

One of the most dangerous areas of work was in munitions. Royal Ordnance Factories tended to be large and sprawling, comprising many small buildings, mostly buried under mounds of earth for protection, in order to keep any explosions small-scale. Work practices were designed to minimise the risk: metal objects, which might cause sparks, were banned, as were matches. The twelve-hour shifts worked by many in factories were seen as far too long for safety – eight hours was the average in munitions. Goggles were provided, though not always worn, as were caps or turbans, and overalls.

ROF badge. The Royal Ordnance Factories produced the munitions for the forces, a vital and dangerous job. As such the workers were on, as the badge says, 'Front Line Duty'.

Long shifts often meant a drop-off in production as shifts dragged on, and it was found that music countered this. Larger concerns would pipe records around the plant's Tannoy system, but many smaller business did not have such systems and in June 1940, the BBC introduced the programme *Music While You Work*, where popular tunes were played. It was found that the tempo of the music would affect the speed at which workers operated, so tunes were chosen for their beat: *Deep In The Heart Of Texas*, which had a clapping section, was banned, as this tended to divert the workers, who joined in. Entertainments National Service Association (ENSA), set up in 1939 to provide concerts for the services, also gave concerts in large factories at lunchtime and other breaks; and in June 1941, the BBC introduced *Worker's Playtime*, to provide such concerts for smaller works.

Factories and businesses had to provide their own ARP teams, particularly fire teams to fight ordinary fires and incendiary bombs. With these in mind, the

first line of defence was the fire watcher, who was tasked with watching for hostile aircraft, anti-aircraft gunfire, bombs falling in the neighbourhood or any other indication of imminent danger of the dropping of incendiaries, and warning the fire teams. Fire watchers were stationed on the roof of their workplace at all times, even when the office or factory was closed. Workers would take turns on duty as fire watchers and fire team members as part of their employment. They were issued with tin helmets and, sometimes, armbands.

By 1943, the production of coal, vital to the war effort, was actually lower than it had been in 1938. This was because mining was not a reserved occupation, and many miners joined the services. By the end of 1943, things had become so serious that the Minister of Labour, Ernest Bevin, ruled that conscripted men could be sent down the mines instead of into the forces. 'Bevin Boys', the name given to these conscripted miners, were chosen by ballot.

Under the Civil Defence Act of July 1939, factories, mines and commercial buildings employing more than thirty persons had to have an ARP scheme, meaning that they had to organise, train and equip ten per cent of their staff into first aid parties, first aid posts, fire parties, rescue squads, and a works' fire brigade equipped with major appliances. In smaller establishments the total numbers involved in ARP could be reduced by the formation of general utility squads, trained in several jobs.

Factories and businesses needed their own ARP teams. This photo shows the fire guards from Lloyd's of London. Note the St John first aid badge worn by the man fourth from right.

"WRONG AGAIN!"

Employers also had to provide shelters, with a warden for every fifty employees or for each shelter. Factory squads were given steel helmets, civilian-duty gas masks, and anti-gas clothing; many larger organisations issued their ARP units with special lapel badges, armbands, and even uniforms.

In 1940, many larger factories and offices formed their own Home Guard units, while members of factory ARP groups also formed auxiliary bomb-disposal units, later attached to the Home Guard, and works' fire brigades, often trained by the national fire service. In all about 150,000 employees were trained in ARP.

As with the official ARP services, when the warning siren went, the ARP workers would put on their helmets and prepare for the raid. Not every warning was followed by a raid, and the loss of production which resulted from false alarms was hugely expensive to the war effort. In September 1940 the Ministry of Home Security introduced the 'industrial warning system', under which the warning siren would only be regarded as an alert. Each factory had a rota of 'roof spotters' – workers trained in aircraft recognition – who, armed with binoculars, warm, weatherproof clothes and tin helmets, were stationed on the roofs, and would sound the alarm if they saw enemy aircraft approaching. Only then would workers go to the shelter. The system, shown to good effect in *Millions Like Us*, proved remarkably effective.

Other women joined the Women's Land Army (WLA), driving tractors, milking cows, making hay, thatching roofs, reclaiming land, herding livestock, catching rats and working in orchards and market gardens. Despite its name, the Land Army was essentially a civilian group and not subject to military discipline. Most members were employed directly by the farmers for whom they worked, and would be paid by them a minimum of £1 2s 6d a week. 'Land Girls' as they were called worked a maximum working week of forty-eight hours in the winter, fifty in the summer.

They were issued with a uniform – brown brogues, brown corduroy or whipcord breeches, fawn knee-length woollen socks, green V-necked pullover, fawn Aertex shirt, brown felt cowboy-style hat, and a tie and armband for formal occasions. For dirty work they had wellingtons, dungarees and an overall coat.

Many of the Land Girls were 'townies' – about a third of the recruits came from London and Middlesex, or from the industrial towns in the north of England. Many female conscientious objectors opted for work in the WLA. In 1942, the WLA Timber Corps was established for forestry work.

Opposite: Humorous postcard; the land girl has tried to milk the bull! Many members of the Women's Land Army were from the towns and cities and had much to learn about farming, but learn they did, winning the respect of most land workers.

SAVE WASTE
AND START A
PIG CLUB

FACTORIES, SCHOOLS, POLICE POSTS, A.R.P. STATIONS— ANY ORGANISED BODY OF INDIVIDUALS CAN HELP THE WAR EFFORT, AND THEMSELVES, BY STARTING A

CO-OPERATIVE
PIG CLUB

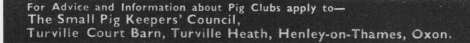

For Advice and Information about Pig Clubs apply to—
The Small Pig Keepers' Council,
Turville Court Barn, Turville Heath, Henley-on-Thames, Oxon.

FOOD AND DRINK

AT THE END OF SEPTEMBER 1939, everyone had to take part in a National Registration, when they were issued with an identity card. The public were told at the time that as well as proving that you were not a German spy, this would be necessary for food rationing. Rationing was not new; during the First World War, German U-boats had tried to impose a stranglehold on Britain's shipping. As food had become short, prices had rocketed. For the better-off, this became a reason for complaint; for the poor it was far more serious, and eventually the government had been forced to bring in a form of rationing.

By the late 1930s Britain was importing twenty million tons of foodstuffs annually, and it was clear that feeding the nation would once again be a real problem in wartime. Almost as soon as war broke out the U-boats were once again busy – there was no 'phoney war' in the Atlantic. Calls immediately began for the government to bring in food rationing – 'fair shares for all' being the slogan. Ration books were sent out from the beginning of October, following national registration, and it was announced that rationing would begin in the new year.

In preparation consumers had to register with a retailer for meat, sugar, butter, bacon and cooking fats; these could either be individual shops or several or all at the same shop. This way, each shop could be issued with the exact amount to supply its registered customers, thus ensuring supply. People still had to pay for the rationed goods – at a maximum price, the government having set or 'controlled' prices for certain goods – but could only receive them (officially) on handing over their ration book.

Food rationing began in January 1940, with each person officially entitled to 4oz butter per week, 12oz sugar and 4oz bacon and ham. Unofficially, there was a 'black market': rationed goods sold at well over the controlled price, but without any coupons involved. A variation on this was the sale of stolen or forged coupons or ration books. All of this was illegal, but most people tolerated it on a small

Opposite: Meat was particularly short during the war. People kept rabbits, chickens and goats in their gardens, while groups were encouraged to form pig clubs.

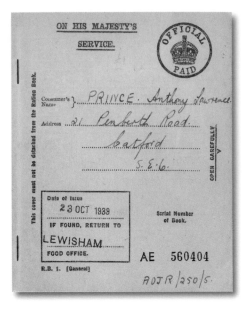

Above: The first food ration books, like this one, were issued in late October 1939, although rationing did not begin until January 1940.

Above right: Unrationed goods such as fish were a good substitute for rationed items like meat. As such they were often sold out.

scale. People sometimes sold their own rations – many poor people could not afford 4oz of bacon or, more often, butter a week, preferring to buy cheaper margarine. Some retailers were left with surplus because not everyone took up their ration, and sold it 'under the counter' to favoured customers. Then there was the 'spiv on the corner', such as *Dad's Army*'s Private Walker, who could always be relied upon for a little bit extra – at a price.

In March 1940, meat was rationed, not by amount, but by value – 1/10d worth per person, per week, except the under-sixes who received 11d worth. This did not include offal, and products such as sausages. Liver, kidneys and heart were seized upon as a way to stretch the rations; as such they soon became difficult to get, and would often be kept to one side for special customers. Onions, too, became a shortage item after the fall of France, and people were encouraged to grow their own.

In July 1940, a national milk scheme was started to encourage children under five to drink milk, by providing a pint of milk a day, either free or at the rate of 2d a pint, depending on the family's circumstances. This also applied to expectant and nursing mothers. What remained after this was shared equally amongst everybody else; about three pints a week each.

As war went on so more items went 'on the ration'; in July, tea at 2oz, margarine and cooking fats. The amount of meat available on the ration also dropped dramatically, to 1 shilling in January 1941, and fish, an obvious alternative, soared in price until it was brought under food control, after which it became hard to get. During 1941, jam, marmalade and syrup went on the ration at a monthly total of 8oz per person, and cheese at just 1oz a week. Vegetarians, including orthodox Jews and Muslims were given extra cheese instead of meat, while agricultural workers, miners and other heavy workers got an extra 8oz. That year a distribution scheme for eggs similar to that for milk was introduced, which meant that an individual might receive only one egg a week, or even three a month. Later 'priority cases' including children, pregnant women, and those with doctor's certificates, would receive four times the normal amount.

Stretching ever-decreasing rations became an ever-increasing headache. Once again advice flowed, especially from the Ministry of Food, which produced leaflets, a radio programme *The Kitchen Front*, short cinema films, and demonstration classes held in local halls. The problem was not so much finding things to eat – there were always potatoes, bread and vegetables – but making them appetising. Flavourings became more important than ever, and people were encouraged to grow their own culinary herbs.

In 1941, the 'Lend-Lease' bill was passed in the USA. Following this food supplies flowed into Britain from America, but never in such consistent amounts that they could be rationed. The answer came in

Far left: The Ministry of Food introduced the milk scheme to ensure that children, the sick, pregnant women and nursing mothers got extra milk.

Left: The Ministry of Food worked hard to produce advice for the housewife on how to make the most of the rations, and how to use 'new' foods from the USA, such as this leaflet on dried eggs.

An old friend goes Vegetarian!

Mock Beefsteak Pudding

Try this for a novel no-meat meal — M°Dougall's own recipe for a Mock Beefsteak Pudding. It has a nourishing filling of savoury vegetables, and what do you think makes that meat pastry crust so perfect? M°Dougall's Self-Raising Flour, of course, the famous flour that a housewife can trust to give her successes every time.

McDougall's

The self-raising flour that gives sure results

RECIPE AND COUPON FOR FREE WARTIME COOKERY BOOK . . . . OVERLEAF

Tight meat rationing meant that vegetarian meals were common, such as this recipe for 'mock beefsteak pudding'.

December with points rationing. As well as the basic rations everybody received a points ration book, which could be used on a range of shortage items, each with its own points value. Points, allocated on a monthly basis, could be used in any shop, rather than a registered supplier. Among the foods available on points were new American goods, such as Spam, Mor (sweetened ham) and soya flour.

Other new foods included powdered eggs and milk (easier to transport than in their natural state), 'national' butter and margarine, and the 'national wholemeal' loaf, introduced to use as much of the wheat as possible. Exotic types of fish also appeared in an attempt to fill the shortages, including snoek (pronounced snook), rock salmon (dogfish), saithe, gurnet, huss, ling and salt cod. Even more alien were whalemeat and horseflesh.

Growing your own food – 'digging for victory' – became a necessity as food supplies dwindled. Flowerbeds and lawns were dug over for growing vegetables, while parks and wasteland were converted to allotments. The moat surrounding the Tower of London was turned over to vegetable growing, but there was an outcry when it was suggested that Wimbledon's tennis courts be dug up. Experienced gardeners were encouraged to help novices, while schools had vegetable gardens tended by pupils as part of the curriculum, with the produce used to supplement school dinners.

The BBC had its share of advice programmes, especially *In Your Garden* with Mr Middleton, and *Radio Allotment*, which followed a group of radio celebrities in their attempts to grow food. Magazines and newspapers carried articles and weekly columns on growing food, and there were a rash of books on all aspects of digging for victory, including keeping chickens, rabbits and goats. Rabbits were seen as a good way to supplement the meat supply, as were goats, which also supplied milk, which could be turned into cheese, while chickens were kept for eggs as well as meat. Groups were encouraged to form 'pig clubs', buying a piglet between them and then rearing it on kitchen waste, etc.

By the end of 1940, fruit was especially short; oranges, if available would be sold 'for children only', bananas were virtually never seen, and carrots were touted as an alternative to fruit, raw, in cakes, or even dipped in toffee as an alternative to toffee apples.

In December 1941, the vitamin welfare scheme started; children under two began to be issued with free cod liver oil and blackcurrant purée, with babies receiving blackcurrant syrup instead. Babies, children, expectant and nursing mothers also received concentrated orange juice, cod liver oil and extra milk. Later, those who could afford it had to pay.

Catering for weddings was an especial problem. Families and friends would club together with their points to buy a few extras, but no amount of points could buy a traditional iced, tiered wedding cake; many hired a fake made from plaster of Paris, with a small drawer at the bottom from which small cubes of fruit cake could be given to the wedding guests.

As victory approached people saved up their coupons for any treats that could be found such as tinned fruit, and the Ministry of Food and magazines were full of suggestions for party food.

If feeding the family proved difficult, feeding the family pets was even worse; there were no rations for them. Leftovers might be used, if there were any, and a small amount of pet food could be bought, though it was difficult to get. Meat judged unfit for human consumption might be got, but even bones were needed for salvage. One recommendation was to put stale bread in the oven until rock hard; this could then be used as dog biscuits, mixed with gravy and a few leftovers. All in all it was a bad time for pets.

WE'VE GOT TO GIVE OF WHAT WE'VE GOT SOMEBODY'S GOT TO FEED YOU LOT!"

Above: As in the First World War, food became short, and to counter this the 'Dig For Victory' scheme was started. Everyone who could, from children to pensioners, was encouraged to grow food.

Left: Catering for wartime weddings, such as this one, was a challenge. Families and friends chipped in with bits of food, or later, points coupons, but they were usually quite spartan affairs.

STITCHCRAFT

8d

Mens Book

SHOPPING AND STYLE

COPING WITH SHORTAGES became one of the common themes on the home front. There were several reasons for these shortages. First, the war-effort demanded huge amounts of raw materials for uniforms, armaments, fuel etc, and these had to be diverted from civilian use. Second, factories which had produced consumer goods increasingly were turned over to war production, while those which did not were hit hardest by the labour shortage as workers were directed into the services or to war-related industries. Last, high employment and shortages generally meant that people had more money to spend, so that what little was available for sale was quickly snapped up. This in itself led to another wartime theme – the queue. People seeing a queue outside a shop would join it without even asking what it was for in the knowledge that at the end of it there was probably something worth having.

The government was keen that this unspent excess cash be put to war use in the form of National Savings; the war was costing vast amounts and the country needed all the money it could get. From 1939 income tax rose to 7s 6d in the pound, then to 8s 6d, then in 1941 to 10s, while purchase tax on 'luxury goods' rose to 100 per cent, yet ever more money was needed.

The War Savings Campaign set about persuading people to buy National Savings Stamps at 6d or 2/6d each – when you had a total of 15s you could exchange them for National Savings Certificates; or for £5 you could buy a 3% Defence Bond. Both of these would give you a guaranteed return after the war. There were also themed savings campaigns, such as the Spitfire Fund, War Weapons weeks, Salute the Soldier weeks, and so on.

At the same time the government tried to curtail unnecessary spending; for this it introduced the 'Squander Bug': a cartoon character of a large insect, with Hitler's face, which tried to talk people into buying things they did not need, thus aiding the enemy.

Opposite: Knitting was one way of supplementing the clothes rations. 'Make do and mend' meant unravelling old knitted garments and re-knitting the old wool, often in the Fair Isle pattern, as demonstrated on this fetching pullover on the cover of this *Stitchcraft* magazine.

Below: The country was spending vast amounts on the war, and the government encouraged saving. Cartoons featuring the 'Squander Bug' demonstrated how unnecessary spending helped the enemy.

Bottom right: The WVS set up children's clothing exchanges across the country where hard-pressed mothers could swap their children's outgrown clothes for larger ones. (IWM D 2088)

Clothes soon became a shortage item, and prices rocketed, so in June 1941, clothing rationing was brought in. This was done on a points basis – everyone received sixty-six coupons, and all items of clothing were given a coupon value. In 1941 this would get a man one overcoat, a three-piece suit, a shirt, a pair of shoes, a set of combinations and a pair of socks. For a woman, an overcoat, a dress, blouse, nightdress, two changes of underwear, a pair of shoes and two pairs of stockings. These are only examples; nearly all clothing was covered by the scheme, and lists of clothes, and their coupon values, were published. In subsequent years these lists would seem more than generous, as annual coupon allocations dropped to sixty, then forty-eight.

Children's clothes required fewer coupons than adults', and children also received extra coupons, but it was still difficult to clothe growing children. You could make your own clothes, however clothing material and knitting wool both required coupons, though not as many as the finished articles. There were ways around this; one was to convert old articles of clothing – 'make do and mend' – and the Board of Trade encouraged this by issuing leaflets, and by organising classes. Knitting was a favourite alternative; old items would be unravelled and re-knitted, often in Fair Isle pattern which, being made up of

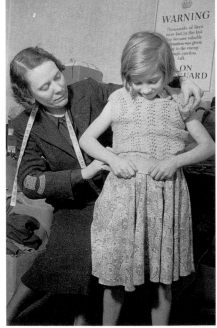

many different colours, was ideal for using up odd bits of yarn. To this end many knitting books were published, showing not just jumpers and scarves, but hats, underwear, ties, stockings, and even the dreaded knitted swimming costume!

Another way to fill a growing child's wardrobe was the old habit of 'hand-me-downs' which, long common in working-class communities, now became everyday for the better-off. To help with this, the WVS set up children's clothing exchanges where a child's wearable, but too small clothes, could be exchanged for bigger items.

Clothes were also subject to government 'austerity' regulations. These laid down strict rules on the amount of cloth and styling that could go into clothes, in order to save material and labour. Women's clothes, for example, could not have more than a set amount of pleats, while men's trousers were not allowed to have turn-ups.

The government introduced the 'utility' scheme, under which clothes were produced to austerity standards. Made to last, utility clothes were free of purchase tax, and therefore doubly attractive, but with few frills and fancies they summed up 1940s austerity. Later the utility scheme would be extended to furniture, crockery, cigarette lighters, and even pencils.

Below left: Clothes rationing was hard for everyone, but particularly the mothers of growing children; even though they received extra coupons it was never enough.

Below: Humorous postcard showing the effects of clothes rationing. The style of the clothing card on the floor dates this card to 1941 – little did they know that things would get much worse!

GOD didn't know
when he made us to grow –
there'd be coupons!

I'm all austerity these days!

45

factory fashion notes

The somewhat glamorous look of the girl on the left was quickly giving way to the far more practical look of the girl on the right; long hair giving way to short, and skirts giving way to trousers.

Opposite top: Women's utility clothing modelled in 1941. The suits, square shoulders, clumpy shoes, and knee-length skirts were all typical of the period. (IWM D 2937)

For women, one of the greatest problems posed by rationing was that of stockings. Two pairs of stockings a year was nowhere near enough. Board of Trade leaflets showed how to make stockings last longer, and how to darn them, but making a pair last six months was impossible. Leg make-up could be applied professionally with the seam at the back painted on as well as the darker bands at the tops of the stocking, but for most it was a DIY affair, with the line up the back done in eyebrow pencil by a friend with a good eye and a steady hand.

By 1941, however, make-up was in short supply. People tried alternatives such as gravy browning, or even gravy powder on the legs, but with little meat for animals you risked being chased down the street by a pack of dogs. In the end most went without, wearing socks, or increasingly trousers, and keeping prized stockings for a special occasion. Other make-up became equally hard to get, and alternatives were tried: beetroot juice for lips, powdered starch for face-powder, boot polish for mascara, soft-lead pencils or dust for eyebrows, and so on. There were also a rash of 'back-street' preparations sold on the black market, with fake containers purporting to be famous brands. Some were poor quality and streaky, others were downright dangerous, containing harmful substances such as lead and arsenic, forcing the Ministry of Information to issue a short film, *Black Market Beauties*, showing the dangers of using such preparations.

The official line was that a clear complexion from eating fresh vegetables, and washing well, was better than make-up. However, this was set back early in 1942, when soap went 'on the ration'. Everybody received four coupons a week, which could be used for toilet soap, hard soap, soap powder or soap flakes, each of which was given a coupon value. Children under twelve months had double coupons, and extra coupons were supplied to those with particularly dirty jobs. The normal monthly ration could get 4oz of household soap or 3oz of toilet soap! As usual there were tips for saving soap, such as keeping soap for as long as possible before using it because hard soap lasts longer than soft; and alternatives: men's shaving soap, for instance, was not rationed, and many women washed their faces with it.

The war brought about a definite look. For men in non-manual jobs, there was a move away from the three-piece suit; the waistcoat went first, replaced by a knitted jumper, usually short-sleeved, often Fair Isle. The trousers tended to wear out faster than the jacket, and rather than buy a new suit at twenty-six coupons, a new pair of trousers, usually non-matching, would do just as well. This led to a slightly shabby, less formal look.

For women there were many more changes. Soap rationing and factory work meant that long hair was a problem, so a much shorter style became the norm, often kept tidy under a headscarf, turban or snood. Trousers, much-frowned upon before the war, became more common than a skirt. And for both men and women patched clothing became almost a sign of honour.

After all this austerity, the arrival of the 'Yanks' in 1942 was a revelation. Unlike the sack-like battledress of the British Tommy the American GI wore a smart 'Ike' jacket, and had seemingly endless supplies of all that was hard to get: cigarettes, soap, nylons and candy – sweets. To the horror of many children, these too were rationed in 1942 – 3oz per person per week – so it was little wonder that US servicemen would be followed by crowds of children, hailing them with the cry 'Got any gum, chum?'

With all this, their exciting new music and dances, such as the jitterbug, and the kind of accents previously only heard at the cinema, it was no wonder that so many British girls found the Americans attractive, and that their male compatriots, especially in the forces, resented them. Fights were common, and the Ministry of Information worked hard to heal the inevitable rifts.

Below: Propaganda poster. In reality they were more likely to be fighting. British men resented the 'Yanks', whom they considered to be 'over-sexed, over-paid and over here'.

"unless we can divide those two fellows –
WE'RE SUNK!"

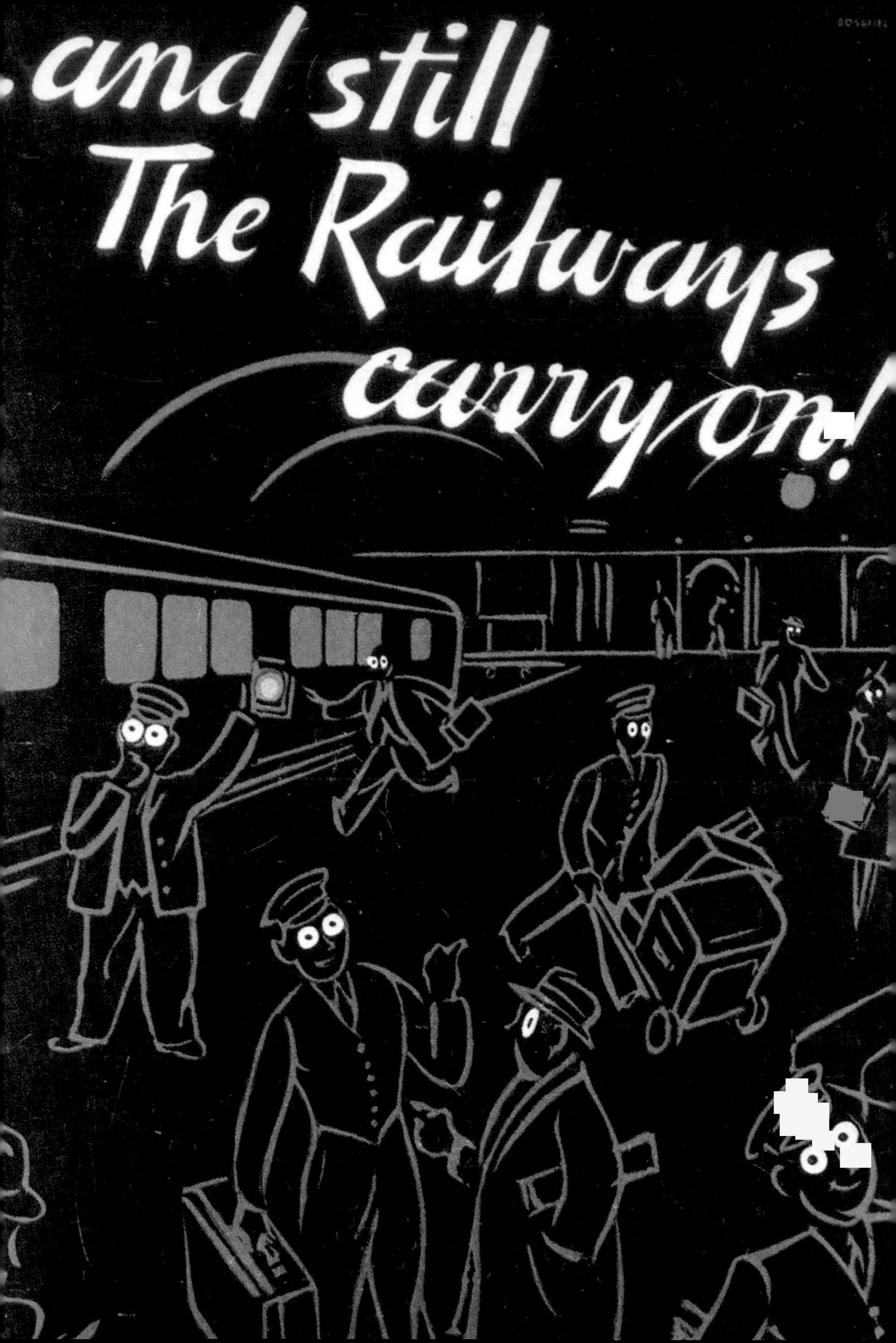
...and still
The Railways
carry on!

TRANSPORT

A T THE BEGINNING OF AUGUST 1939, the government announced that petrol would be rationed in the advent of war, although it was not actually introduced until 23 September. Until then there were queues of drivers at garages, trying to stock up on petrol, filling not only their cars but every conceivable container. One week before rationing, branded petrol was replaced by 'pool' petrol, at a controlled price of 1s 6d a gallon; pool petrol was a national blend, and many drivers complained that it caused 'pinking', a knocking sound in the engine.

To receive their ration book, car owners had to take their registration book to their local post office. The ration given to each motorist depended on their car's horsepower and allowed for about 200 miles of motoring a month, varying from four to ten gallons per month. Additional petrol might be granted if your car use was essential to the war effort or the life of the community, such as a doctor or commercial travellers. Motorcyclists also received a small petrol ration.

Motoring associations and the press gave advice for getting the best out of your car, such as maintaining an even speed, and free-wheeling down hills. One common – though illegal – way of stretching your petrol was to add paraffin or creosote to it, or even to run your car on paraffin alone, although this made a terrible smell, and produced clouds of smoke. There were a rash of inventions on sale, many of them dubious, which were 'guaranteed' to increase mileage.

One of the more successful of these was gas power. For about £30 – quite a lot of money in 1939 – cars and vans could be converted to run on ordinary coal gas. This meant having an auxiliary carburettor fitted and carrying a gas-bag in a wooden cradle about nine feet by six feet by four feet high on the car's roof. Although bulky, the bag did not add much to the car's weight; it was, however, only capable of holding the equivalent of a gallon of petrol, thus needing frequent

Opposite: The blackout affected railway travel too. Especially when station name-boards were taken down as part of anti-invasion measures in 1940.

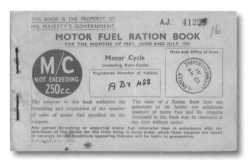

Petrol ration book for 1941. Petrol was rationed, the amount depending upon the engine capacity of the car or, in this case, motorcycle.

The dangers of blackout driving. This car in Bristol has driven straight into a bomb crater.

re-filling, a job which took about ten minutes. However, the shortage of fuel in general meant that conversions were banned in October 1942, and existing gas-driven vehicles could only be used if they were employed on essential work.

A black market soon sprang up in petrol. Non-coupon petrol could be bought for about 6s–7s a gallon from people who had built up a stockpile, and when this ran out red-dyed commercial petrol soon found its way onto the private market. Police 'dipped' the tanks of suspect cars, and the black market responded by finding ways of removing the dye. Another lucrative black market trade was in stolen or forged coupons.

Late in 1940 a 'free lifts' scheme was brought in; window stickers were provided and motorists displaying such a sticker got extra petrol. One year later the basic ration was cut to a monthly average of 125 miles; and in July 1942 the basic ration was stopped altogether, and only those on government business were allowed any petrol at all.

The blackout regulations brought in on 1 September 1939 included traffic. Those driving or cycling at night had to dim and screen lights. Cars could use sidelights only, with the glass covered by two thicknesses of newspaper. Streetlights were turned off, and traffic lights either masked to leave just a small cross of each colour, or fitted with hoods.

All these restrictions made driving almost impossible, so white paint was used liberally. Roads were painted with a continuous white line along the centre of the carriageway, while kerbs at road junctions, intersections, roundabouts, bends and corners were pained with white dashes, and trees and lamp-posts bordering roads were painted in six-inch horizontal bands from ground level to a height of three feet. Cars also had to have their bumpers and running-boards painted white.

Within a week the use of the offside headlamp, heavily

dimmed, was allowed, and soon an official blackout mask for car headlamps was available, becoming compulsory from January 1940. Side and rear lamps also had to be covered, with the reflectors painted matt black.

Strict blackout rules applied equally to bicycles, which had to carry a white front lamp, red rear lamp, and have a six-inch length of the rear mudguard painted white.

In spite of the huge drop in car travel due to petrol rationing, the number of road deaths, particularly among child pedestrians, increased, and in November 1939 a maximum speed limit of 20mph was brought in for built-up areas during the blackout.

From the summer of 1940 numerous Home Guard roadblocks were set up, at which identity cards had to be shown, posing yet another frustration for the private motorist. In some areas these might be encountered every few miles, and tempers were sorely tested.

The blackout, designed to make life difficult for enemy bombers, had the same effect on people who had to go out at night, although like much else, after a while people got used to it.

A large drop in the use of private cars meant a surge in the use of public transport. The result was queues and overcrowding. The government tried to cut down unnecessary use with campaigns exhorting people to 'walk short distances' and asking 'Is your journey really necessary?' Offices and factories were asked to stagger their starting times, and housewives were encouraged to shop after the morning rush hour. Queue-jumping caused arguments and from April 1942, queuing became law. If six or more people were waiting for a bus they had to 'form and keep a queue or line of not more than two abreast on the footway'.

Some buses went over to what was termed 'producer gas'. Under this method the vehicle towed behind it a trailer carrying an anthracite burner rather like a large dustbin, which produced gas, which in turn powered the bus, giving it a range of up to 150 miles. By early 1942, seventy-five firms, including many bus companies, were making use of this method. The drawbacks were that the vehicles proved difficult

to drive, needed a lot of maintenance, and were far less powerful than petrol models, often finding steep hills impossible to negotiate. From 1943, petrol supplies for commercial companies were improved, and most companies converted their gas-producing buses back to petrol.

At the beginning of September 1939 the four main railway companies, several smaller ones and the London Passenger Transport Company were placed under the direct control of the Minister of Transport, forming a sort of early national transport.

The blackout applied equally to the railways; no lights at all were allowed in carriages, but as with the roads, there was soon some relaxation, with a small light thrown onto each seat by a central fitting. Should the warning sound, all carriage lights were switched off, and the train would continue to the next station where it would stop to let passengers go to a shelter if they wanted. Until it got there, passengers were advised to pull down the blinds to prevent injury from flying glass, and sit or lie on the floor. Like all other forms of public transport, the trains became ever more crowded – by 1944 passenger trains were carrying more than twice as many passengers as before the war – and getting a seat was a luxury; and as for lying on the floor – impossible!

Travelling on London's Underground also became a trial, not only due to overcrowded carriages, but because the platforms would begin to fill up with shelterers from late afternoon. Placards were put up in stations to inform

Top: The blackout could be far more than just a nuisance. Switching off the streetlights and severely reducing the light emitted by car headlamps meant that pedestrians could hardly be seen, and death rates rose dramatically.

Bottom: Petrol rationing meant that public transport use soared, leading to severe overcrowding. Housewives were encouraged to do their shopping outside of the rush hour to cut down the queues.

passengers emerging from the Underground if the air raid warning had been sounded.

On railway stations, all the lights would be put out at the sound of the warning, making it difficult for travellers to know if they had reached a station or if the train had merely come to a halt. In June 1940, as an anti-invasion measure, station name-boards were painted over or removed altogether, making life more difficult than ever for travellers who were advised, if they knew the line, to tell fellow passengers where they were. Porters would call out the name of the station, and platform edges were painted white.

And after all this, the chance of refreshment was low; even in stations, a shortage of cups and glasses meant that passengers were advised to bring their own. Restaurant cars on trains became a rarity, and by mid-1944 they had disappeared entirely.

Bicycles were one answer to crowded public transport, and as such prices, even of the most dilapidated second-hand bike, shot up. One difficulty became replacing tyres and inner tubes as rubber went into shortage after the Japanese invasion of Malaya. A response to this was the introduction of synthetic rubber inner tubes.

One type of freight transport, the canal boat, saw a renaissance as the roads and railways became more crowded; with one new element: often they were 'manned' by the new type of worker – women. Conversely the docks were hard-hit. As the gateways for Britain's vital imports they were prime targets for air raids.

Top: Petrol rationing. A London Transport bus towing its own gas generator plant. Buses run on these gas generators were slow and found hills difficult.

Bottom: Canals had a fresh lease of life, with many narrow boats and barges being handled, like this one, by women.

Overleaf: Street scene in 1941. The warning sirens have just sounded and the air raid wardens and the policeman are directing people into the basement public shelter. Only a few people are carrying gas masks, as after the first few weeks of war most people did not. Note the white lines on the road, kerbs, lamppost and car, all to aid visibility in the blackout, and the blackout masks on the car headlight, traffic lights, and illuminated shelter sign. (Artwork by Christa Hook)

Relaxation and
Entertainment

By the late 1930s the main Victorian forms of public entertainment, the music hall, the theatre and the concert hall, were still in existence (the music hall having mainly changed into variety theatre), but were quickly making way for their more modern offspring, the cinema, the radio, or more properly the wireless, and newest of all, the television.

Regular public broadcasting of television (to the London area only) began in November 1936. At around 80 guineas sets were expensive, but by the outbreak of war the cost was quickly falling and there were about 20,000 sets in use. Yet television would play no part in the war, as broadcasting closed down on 1 September 1939 'for the duration of the emergency'. It was argued that enemy aircraft could use the television signal as a homing beam; but also closure would release many skilled engineers and technicians, who were desperately needed for the war effort.

When Neville Chamberlain announced that 'this country is at war with Germany' on BBC radio, the audience was huge; in 1939, nine million licences were issued representing about ninety per cent of the households in the country.

Since the time of Munich the BBC had been preparing for war. The wireless would be vital to give the public information, advice and instructions; it was therefore vital that bombing would not break the flow of information, creating panic.

The answer was to shut down the eight separate BBC channels broadcast before the war, and to produce a single channel, broadcast from transmitters around the country. Thus the Home Service was born on the same evening that television was shut down. It was not a great start, broadcasting information rather than entertainment; news bulletins every hour, interspersed with official notices, instructions, regulations and exhortations. Between these were programmes of gramophone records and for long periods, Sandy MacPherson at the

Opposite: The 'wireless' was at its height during the war; people listened for news and information, or to escape the war with entertainment or music. Television was banned 'for the duration', but it would return with a vengeance.

Arthur Askey

Arthur Askey – 'Big-hearted Arthur', star of the war's first comedy hit, *Band Waggon*. It was also the first wireless comedy programme; there had been comedians before, but always as part of a variety show.

ITMA, the most popular wireless show of the war, was full of catchphrases such as 'don't forget the diver!'. They caught the nation's imagination, so much so that postcards such as this were issued.

organ. All this was aimed at a short, but violent conflict, which did not actually happen.

The BBC was evacuated with 'variety' and the music department going to Bristol, the religious department going to Bedford, and the drama department to Evesham. Local halls were hastily converted into studios and within days something like pre-war broadcasting was returning.

It was soon realised that most people wanted to be entertained; light music, variety and comedy were favourites, with the most remembered wartime shows being comedy programmes. One of the best loved was *Band Waggon* with Arthur Askey, Richard "Stinker" Murdoch and Sid Walker. Its first wartime broadcast was on 16 September 1939. *BandWaggon* was the first radio show to use catchphrases in a big way including 'Big-hearted Arthur that's me', 'hello playmates', 'ah happy days' and 'you silly little man'. It only lasted until December 1939, but was very influential. Other popular shows included *Garrison Theatre* with Jack Warner – 'mind my bike', *Much Binding in the Marsh, Hi Gang* starring the American couple Ben Lyon and Bebe Daniels with Vic Oliver, and *Happidrome*.

The biggest radio show of the war was undoubtedly *ITMA*, starring Tommy Handley. Like *BandWaggon*, it had started pre-war, as *It's That Man Again*, but Handley changed it to *ITMA* to give it a wartime slant as everything now seemed to have military acronyms. Full of absurd

AN ITMA WISECRACK — *illustrated by Bert Thomas*

"Don't forget the Diver!"

characters: Colonel Chinstrap, Mrs Mopp, Ally Oop, the German spy Funf, and many more, led of course by the 'Minister of Aggravation and Mysteries', Handley himself, *ITMA* was a sea of catchphrases; 'Can I do you now, Sir?', 'This is Funf speaking', 'I go – I come back', and 'don't forget the diver' among many. It ran throughout the war and it was said that the Royal family were only to be disturbed for the most pressing news when *ITMA* was on.

The BBC did not escape the Blitz. On 16 October 1940, Broadcasting House received a direct hit and six people were killed. Bruce Belfrage was reading the news when listeners heard the sound of a bomb exploding in the background, but after a brief pause Belfrage continued with the bulletin. A few months later, after a second bomb strike, part of the building had to be evacuated. On both occasions, programmes continued on schedule.

It's that man himself – Tommy Handley, the 'Minister of Aggravation and Mysteries', who presided over the madness of *ITMA* throughout the war.

A few months before, the name Bruce Belfrage, or Alvar Liddell, or of any of the newsreaders, would have been virtually unknown, as news bulletins only started with 'Here is the news from London'; but after the fall of France, when there were fears of Nazi paratroops seizing the BBC, or of spoof transmissions, the newscasters changed to 'here is the news and this is Freddy Grisewood [or whoever] reading it'. One surprise favourite personality was from Germany; Lord Haw Haw, in reality William Joyce, who would start his broadcasts 'Germany [pronounced 'Jairmany'] calling, Germany calling.' His propaganda programmes, designed to strike fear into the hearts of the British, became almost universal listening.

'Uncle Mac', Dennis McCulloch, continued to introduce the daily *Children's Hour,* with his famous line; 'Hello children everywhere', although it was now only half an hour long. There were also two daily broadcasts for schools, which were a particular godsend to those children who had no school to go to.

The music show *Yours* with Vera Lynn, was a particular favourite, especially with the British forces abroad, earning her the nickname 'the Forces' Sweetheart.' Other hit programmes included Mr Middleton's *In Your Garden*, and *The Brains Trust*, where a team of intellectuals would discuss questions and problems sent in by the listeners.

One last surprise hit was the King's Christmas speech. There had been a couple of these prior to 1939, but they were not done every year. In 1939, George VI, who had a speech impediment, was convinced, reluctantly, that a Christmas speech to his people would

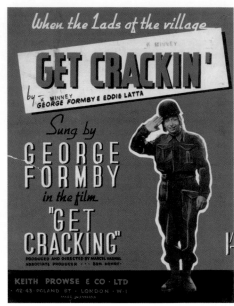

Above: 'The Forces' Sweetheart' Vera Lynn, produced a wireless programme for the forces, named after this song.

Top right: George Formby was the biggest box-office draw at the cinema for the first years of the war, starring in a series of home front roles, such as this one, in which he plays a member of the village Home Guard.

be good for morale. It was a huge success, which he was prevailed upon to repeat in 1940 and subsequent years, until it became an annual tradition.

During the war cinema-going was at its all-time high in Britain. At first, many of the films produced in Britain were flag-wavers such as *The Lion Has Wings* (1939), *One of Our Aircraft is Missing* (1942), and *Went The Day Well?* (1942), but most popular with the public were more escapist fare, including American films such as *Gone With The Wind* (1939) and *Dumbo* (1941). The top box-office star during the first half of the war was George Formby, who starred in a string of musical comedies including *Let George do it* (1940), *Turned Out Nice Again* (1941), *Much Too Shy* (1942) and *Get Cracking* (1943).

The government had initially closed down cinemas and theatres, arguing that should one be bombed, the casualties could be horrendous. After a few days, following a general outcry, they backed down, but patrons had to be told if an air raid warning was sounded, usually with a slide flashed up on the screen, and asked to leave quietly if they wished to take cover, with the show continuing for those who wanted to carry on watching. At first, many cinemas and theatres carried signs stating 'No patrons admitted without gas masks', although these tended to disappear after the first few weeks as no gas was used, and most people ceased to carry their masks.

As well as the big film, shows would include a newsreel, and often some government shorts on Dig for Victory, make do and mend, food tips, or ARP matters. At first these were very stodgy, official-type affairs, which were often greeted with whistles and cat-calls, but the Ministry of Information soon began to use cartoons and humour to make them more entertaining and less 'preachy'.

Above: An ENSA concert party. Such groups toured camps, factories and halls to entertain both the forces and civilians.

Below: Lunchtime concerts of classical music at London's National Gallery were a regular attraction during the war.

Dances were another very common entertainment, and typically would be advertised at 'half price for members of HM forces in uniform'. Many large factories would organise dances, as would military bases, and locals or members of the military would be bussed in, in an attempt to provide enough dance partners. With the arrival of the US forces, the dances tended to be far more lively, with dances such as the jitterbug being introduced.

Concerts were common; ENSA – dubbed by some as 'Every Night Something Awful' – was set up in 1939 by Basil Dean and Leslie Henson. ENSA concert parties would be given in factories, military bases and in local halls. As well as entertaining the troops or the workers, these were an important part of local fund-raising events, and would be in 'Holiday at Home Week' programmes. Holiday at Home Weeks were an attempt to curb travel by encouraging people to stay at home during their annual holiday, and these programmes were designed to replace the 'end of the pier' shows popular at the seaside. All sorts of groups, including the ARP, the fire service, Scouts and Guides, would have their own concert parties, as well as professional groups.

Some of the most prestigious of music concerts were those at London's National Gallery. These lunchtime concerts, in aid of the musicians' benevolent fund, included artists such as Dame Myra Hess, Benjamin Britten, and Geraint Jones.

EDUCATION AND
SOCIAL SERVICE

THE WAR was to have a great effect on education. In the last days before war was declared the evacuation of children from the cities, industrial towns, and ports of Britain to safer areas began. Most children went with their schools; under plans worked out in the early thirties it had been recognised that the most efficient way of moving millions of children was by school group. In this way the parents could be easily informed, practices arranged; and, as the children would be accompanied by their teachers, they would know and be known by those who would be in charge of them.

On 1 September, the first school groups from the evacuation areas set out, using trains, buses, trams, coaches, and even pleasure steamers to take them to the reception areas. On arrival the children were billeted with local families, and in many cases the schools would share buildings with the local school. This was done by splitting the day into two, with the local school occupying the building in the morning and the evacuated school taking over in the afternoon, or vice versa. Often this would be rotated weekly.

In other places there was no suitable local school building; here buildings such as church halls or even barns were adapted for the purpose. In the case of some private schools, they had made their own 'twinning' arrangements with local private schools to share buildings.

To encourage parents to send their children with their school group, most school buildings in evacuation areas were closed. In the event, only about a third of those children due to be evacuated actually went, and those who stayed behind had an extended holiday. Slowly, however, some schools re-opened, although others were turned into auxiliary fire stations or ARP depots. Over the next few months those pupils who had stayed behind were joined by others drifting back from evacuation as the expected air raids failed to materialise.

As the war went on there would be more large-scale evacuations, first as invasion threatened, then with the start of the Blitz, and finally

Opposite: Mothers of younger children were often evacuated with their children. Here a group assembles at the station before catching the train. (IWM HU 36237)

September 1939.
Schools in the
danger areas
were evacuated,
with groups of
children making
their way to the
safety of the
countryside.
(IWM HU 36238)

Gas mask drill.
Children in
schools would
regularly have
drills in
preparation for
the feared poison
gas attacks.
Notice the range
of boxes and
cases, and the boy
giving the
wartime 'salute'
of the thumbs up.
(IWM HU 3162)

with the V-weapon attacks of 1944–5. After each wave of evacuation there would be a drift back, and as numbers declined, so the remaining evacuees would be integrated into local schools.

Schools were affected by the shortages that applied to other facets of wartime life. Everything from textbooks to paper and pencils was in short supply and a great deal of sharing took place. Life changed in other ways: air raid shelters were dug in school fields, or cellars strengthened and adapted. Even in the 'phoney war' period, gas mask drills were common, as were air raid drills. In the first, the teacher would blow their whistle, and the children would put on their masks and carry on working, so as to get used to wearing them. In an air raid drill, children would line up, then walk in crocodile file out to the shelter. Later these drills would become the real thing; lessons would carry on in the shelter and many schools found that the noise of the raids could be drowned out by chanting tables, or better, by singing, and sometimes the piano was moved into the shelter to aid this.

With the advent of the V-1, or 'doodlebug', which could come over at any time, many schools arranged rotas of pupils to act as V-1 watchers. On seeing one approaching the school they would give the alarm, and the pupils would duck under their desks, another thing regularly practiced.

Some schools were hit, often at night when they were empty, but sometimes there were casualties, as when Sandhurst Road School in

At Sandhurst Road School in Catford, thirty-eight children and six teachers were killed when it was hit by a 'tip-and-run' raider at lunchtime on 20 January 1943.

A family portrait showing some of the range of war duties people carried out. The sister on the left is in the green uniform of the Women's Voluntary Service, and the sister on the right is an ARP driver. Their brother is an RAF air gunner.

Catford, south-east London was hit one lunchtime, with the loss of thirty-eight children and six teachers.

School meals, unusual before the war, became the norm as mothers were encouraged to work, and school milk was introduced as part of the Ministry of Food's welfare scheme. Small remote schools were supplied by the WVS with meals cooked at central canteens. To help with the war effort pupils were encouraged to buy savings stamps, take part in salvage schemes – collecting paper, metal, rags or bones – and to Dig for Victory.

The WVS was one of many women's organisations, such as Women's Institutes, which played a vital part on the home front. However the WVS was formed expressly in response to the situation facing Britain. The Women's Voluntary Services for ARP was started in June 1938. It was founded by the Dowager Marchioness of Reading, Stella Isaacs, to recruit women to the civil defence services, but it soon became far more than that. From early on, it took on the slogan 'the WVS never says no', and this describes the wartime work of the group, who could be relied upon to take on any new job that didn't quite fit into the remit of any other group.

In 1938–39 the WVS mainly recruited and trained women for ARP and the Land Army. In 1939 and 1940 their main work was evacuation – billeting, communal feeding, and clothing. In September 1939, members in reception areas found places for evacuees, while others accompanied groups of evacuees from the cities and helped to iron out the problems which confronted them. With the coming of the Blitz in 1940, they set up story corners for toddlers in public shelters, and did post-raid welfare work. When war work for women became compulsory they gave women advice about factory work and ran day nurseries for the children of factory workers and residential nurseries for young evacuees. By 1943 their energies were chiefly directed to National Savings, make do and mend and salvage. One WVS scheme, the cog scheme, involved children in the collection of salvage, and badges were awarded to the keenest collectors.

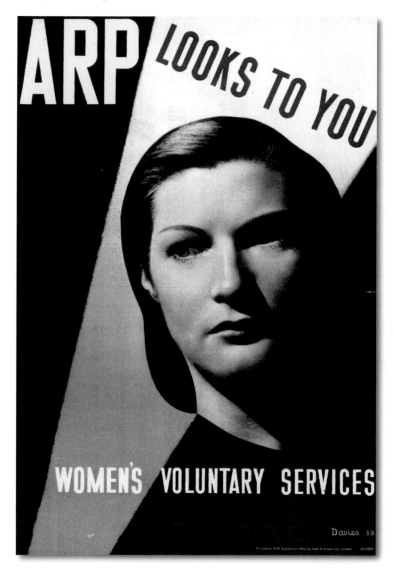

The first task of the WVS was to recruit women for the ARP services, using posters such as this one.

Communal feeding was a major area for the WVS. They ran mobile canteens to serve civil defence units at the site of incidents, as well as military units stationed in remote parts, merchant seamen, building workers, schoolchildren and evacuees. Mobile library services run by the WVS also catered for their minds.

In 1941 Middlesex County Council asked the WVS to staff emergency feeding units, like army field kitchens; the scheme soon spread across the country. Mobile versions of these, the 'Queen's Messenger Convoys', were used for the emergency feeding of large groups of civilians affected by bombing in such places as Coventry, and were almost entirely staffed by WVS members.

Another problem was how to provide a midday meal for people working full-time on the land, including the Land Army. The WVS responded by providing them with savoury pies. Besides farm workers, they supplied village schools, small factories and workmen on remote sites. These are only some of the jobs carried out by the WVS, the Women's Institutes, the Salvation Army, the Girl Guides and other voluntary organisations during the war, but they give a flavour of the important tasks they performed.

A 'Food Flying Squad' mobile canteen. These were part of the Queen's Messenger Convoys which supplied hot food and drinks to heavily raided areas. That this is such an area can be seen from the damaged roofs and windows of the houses in the background. (IWM HU 49498)

Rest centres were set up for those bombed out of their homes. This is an armband issued to rest centre staff, many of whom were WVS members.

It was recognised before the war that the main cause of distress to those on the home front in a war would be bombing. Those injured were to be dealt with by hospitals and first aid centres, but there would also be the problem of those made homeless. A scheme was prepared for the provision of 'rest and feeding shelters', intended to accommodate people for 24 to 48 hours, after which time they would have been billeted by the local authority.

In the event, although the bombing was severe, there were far fewer deaths than expected, and far more made homeless – during the Blitz of 1940–41 over a third of a million lost their homes. To lessen the problem, people were advised to make arrangements in advance to move in with friends or relatives in the event of being made homeless; but this was not always possible, and the answer was the rest centre.

Cinemas, halls, schools, all sorts of buildings were turned into emergency rest centres. Services provided included information desks, first aid, and nursery corners. A small amount of money might be given out to those in greatest need, and clothes, replacement ration books and identity cards issued. When alternative accommodation was found, furniture would be needed. The WVS organised a scheme for the collection of all sorts of household goods to be distributed to those who had been bombed out.

Animals weren't forgotten. The National ARP for Animals Committee was set up to prevent and reduce animal suffering as a result of raids. If an animal was injured, or dug out of the rubble, the wardens or police would report it to a NARPAC animal steward, who would call in, if necessary, a vet or slaughterman. NARPAC also ran a scheme for animal registration, where they issued numbered collar tags for pets, so that they could be reunited with their owners if they became separated.

HEALTH

AT A TIME when many people were working either directly or indirectly as part of the war effort, being healthy became a vital part of that war effort. It was seen as a duty to stay healthy and fit, and not take time off work. A lot of information was given to the public on various basic themes such as eating well and getting exercise.

Eating well meant having a balanced diet made up of 'foods for warmth and energy', such as sugar, bread, fats; 'builders and repairers'; proteins such as meat, fish, cheese and dairy products; and 'protective foods'; dairy products, fish and fresh fruit and vegetables. The Ministry of Food worked hard to give advice to the housewife on providing balanced meals, but in the end this was mostly achieved by the rationing system. Much of the food which was hard to get, or rationed, was unhealthy in large amounts: meat, butter, fats, sugar, sweets, biscuits, cream and so on. What was freely available was good for you: fresh vegetables, wholemeal bread, etc. On top of that, alcohol was short, as were cigarettes.

For those who needed extra vitamins etc (young children, pregnant women and the sick), there was the welfare scheme. In April 1940, Lord Woolton became minister of food, he was determined that rationing should 'stamp out the diseases that arose from malnutrition, especially those amongst children, such as rickets'. That July the national milk scheme was started to encourage children under five to drink milk, by providing a pint of milk a day, either free or, to those who could afford it, at 2d a pint. The same applied to expectant and nursing mothers. In April 1941, they were joined by 'invalids', who, with a doctor's certificate got either seven or fourteen pints a week. Only after these priority groups had been supplied would what remained be divided up for general sale.

Exercise and fresh air were regarded as a must, especially for those who worked long hours in offices. Weekend cycling tours were recommended, as was hiking, while the BBC introduced *The Daily Dozen*,

Opposite: ARP first aid parties were formed to deal with casualties on the spot at 'incidents'. Here, casualty workers are practising for just such an event.

Below: With an
acute manpower
shortage, it was
essential for the
nation to keep fit
and stay fit.
Spreading illnesses
was a sin.

Below right:
Poster for the
welfare service. In
spite of shortages
it was thought
essential for
children to be
given the vitamins
and minerals they
needed to grow
fit and strong. To
this end milk, cod
liver oil and
orange juice were
issued free to
those who
needed them.

"My first aid was indispensable. If I hadn't put my
head between my knees, I'd have fainted . . . !"

W. FAUKES

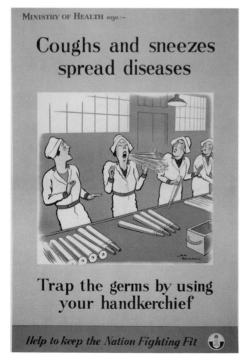

MINISTRY OF HEALTH says:—

Coughs and sneezes spread diseases

Trap the germs by using your handkerchief

Help to keep the Nation Fighting Fit

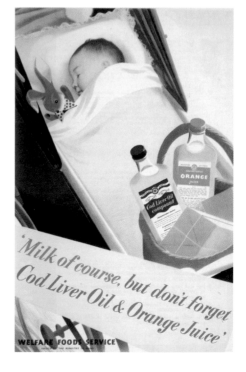

'Milk of course, but don't forget
Cod Liver Oil & Orange Juice'

WELFARE FOODS SERVICE

a short radio programme of exercises to join in with, split, interestingly, into exercises for men and for women. For many, however, petrol rationing and the difficulties of public transport meant that the daily journey to work was often carried out on foot, meaning that the government's exhortations to 'use shanks's pony' and 'avoid unnecessary journeys' were unnecessary. Added to the better diet and the shortages of alcohol and tobacco, this meant that people were generally fitter than they had been pre-war.

Opposite top: First aid classes, booklets and pamphlets were widely available to the public, as this cartoon demonstrates.

How to keep well in Wartime

ISSUED FOR THE MINISTRY OF HEALTH BY THE MINISTRY OF INFORMATION

The Ministry of Health worked hard to keep the nation 'fighting fit', issuing advice in advertisements, short films and booklets such as this one

'Hitler's Follies', the staff of a heavily sand-bagged First Aid Post early in the war. Here, people with minor injuries were treated, easing the load on the hospitals.

In 1939 it was considered that the main health problem connected to the home front would be the vast numbers of dead and injured caused by enemy attack. As war approached, 200,000 beds were reserved for air raid casualties, this space being made by emptying asylums and sanitoria; sending the patients unexpectedly back to their relatives. Just before the outbreak of war, for instance, eight thousand tuberculosis patients were sent home and told not to cough over young people. In other places, country mansions were requisitioned for use as hospitals.

In spite of this, it was still feared that hospitals might be overwhelmed by casualties, so a triage system was to be operated. 'First aid parties', trained by the British Red Cross Society, the St Andrew's Ambulance Corps and the St John Ambulance Brigade, would go directly to bombing incidents, where they would ease the strain on the hospitals by dealing with minor casualties on the spot. Casualties who needed further treatment but were able to make their own way to a 'first aid post', could be directed to do so by a member of the first aid party. This would leave only casualties who needed to be driven to first aid posts or clearing hospitals.

First aid posts were designed for the treatment of casualties who needed to be seen by a doctor, but who would probably be able to go home after treatment. For this purpose, every first aid post had at least one medical officer and one trained nurse, while a high proportion of the staff were women, many of them nursing auxiliaries. Posts were usually set up in specially adapted and equipped buildings. People injured at work or at home might also go to a first aid post for emergency treatment. For use in less densely populated areas, there were mobile first aid posts, which had a skeleton staff, equipment and suitable transport.

Few air raid shelters, public or private, were comfortable, and dampness and cold were common problems, leading to colds and coughs, so that the terms 'shelter cough', 'shelter throat' and 'shelter flu' were commonly used. Many people used public shelters, either because they had no shelter of their own or because they felt more secure surrounded by other people. However, one of the added drawbacks of the communal shelter was infection. This not only included illnesses; lice, too, were a danger. One warden wrote that they were usually brought in by tramps who, by using the shelter, were saving the shilling that a Salvation Army hostel would have cost them. The authorities tried to counter this; first they introduced 'isolation bays' in shelters, and shelter marshals, whose job it was to keep order in the shelters, had to try to coax or cajole people to sit there.

A public shelter. Notice the rather rudimentary toilet arrangement. There was a great deal of concern about the unhealthy conditions in the public shelters. (IWM D 1601)

As night raiding became the norm, the shift to what was called 'dormitory shelters' exacerbated the problem. In September 1940, a committee chaired by Lord Horder was appointed to look into the conditions of air raid shelters used for sleeping purposes, with particular reference to health.

The committee made its initial recommendations just four days after it was set up. Its written report was wide-ranging, recommending the provision of amenities such as lighting and bunks, and the means of hanging entrance curtains on doors. Regular inspections should be made by the medical officer of health, and local authorities authorised to provide adequate sanitary equipment within shelters, ensure regular cleansing of the shelters and dispose of the contents of the toilets. In terms of the spread of disease, the committee felt that the risk of airborne infection might be reduced by the use of disinfectant sprays, while compulsory powers should be given to delouse any shelterers thought to be a threat to others.

Most of these recommendations were quickly taken up. The committee also recommended the use of a facemask by shelterers which could be privately purchased – few took this up.

A poster warning of the dangers of the 'easy' girl-friend. The possibility of death at any moment led to a loosening of morals, and a sharp increase in venereal disease.

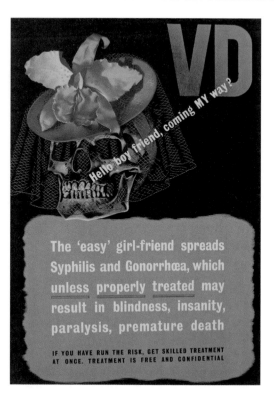

The 'easy' girl-friend spreads Syphilis and Gonorrhœa, which unless properly treated may result in blindness, insanity, paralysis, premature death

IF YOU HAVE RUN THE RISK, GET SKILLED TREATMENT AT ONCE. TREATMENT IS FREE AND CONFIDENTIAL

In London and other places, rules were issued for the public shelters, including one that you should not 'enter if suffering from an infectious illness, in which case shelterers may be asked to leave'. Later the government issued regulations, including one stating that 'people who are not clean, or who have an infectious disease, are not allowed to sleep in public shelters.'

The vagrants struck back: at the capital's Charing Cross Station, fifty vagrants took over one of the lesser-used arch shelters in Hungerford Lane which became a sort of alternative shelter for London's rough-sleepers. In the end the authorities gave in and transformed another of the arches into a combined air raid shelter, cleansing station and welfare centre, installing baths, bunks, a canteen and a first aid post.

B.T. 27.

For he to-day that sheds his Blood with me
Shall be my Brother *Henry. V.*

The blood which you so generously gave has been used by the fighting forces. This brings you the thanks of those concerned for the personal service you have rendered to your country.

ARMY BLOOD TRANSFUSION SERVICE

Charles Thomas

Blood-transfusion card. Mobile transfusion squads toured the country collecting blood in factories, offices, pit-heads and halls, for use in hospitals at home and at the front.

There was one other, surprising rule for public shelters: in the interests of public health, 'smoking should be prohibited in public shelters except where a separate compartment can be set aside for smokers.' Even Winston Churchill, that famous cigar smoker, was ordered to put one out when carrying out an inspection tour of a shelter!

One particular infectious disease reared its head during the war – venereal disease (VD). The war saw an alarming increase in the spread of VD as the blackout made the prostitute's job far easier, with many carrying out business in the now dark alleyways, while the possibility of death at any moment led to an almost inevitable relaxation of morals amongst many. By the last years of the war, posters and adverts in newspapers referred openly to a problem previously not mentioned in polite circles.

The war also saw the spread of a relatively new medical service; blood transfusion. Blood had been transferred between people for some time, but it had only recently been realised that a store of blood could speed the process and save lives. Mobile blood-transfusion groups toured the cities and villages of Britain, collecting blood that would save countless lives on the home and battle fronts.

In 1942, the Beveridge Committee began to look at post-war social provision. Amongst other things their report would recommend the formation of a national health system and a department of social security. The course of post-war welfare was set.

PLACES TO VISIT

Visitors are advised to check opening times before travelling.

Bletchley Park, The Mansion, Bletchley Park, Milton Keynes, MK3 6EB.
  Telephone: 01908 640404.
  (Britain's code-breaking centre; several displays on home front life.)
Chiselhurst Caves, Old Hill, Chislehurst, Kent, BR7 5NL.
  Telephone: 020 8467 3264.
  (Good example of local caves used as a massive public air raid shelter.)
Churchill War Rooms, Clive Steps, King Charles Street, London SW1A 2AQ.
  Telephone: 020 7930 6961.
  (Britain's underground control centre.)
Clifford Road Air Raid Shelter Museum, Clifford Road Primary School,
  Clifford Road, Ipswich, Suffolk, IP4 1PJ. Telephone: 01473 251605.
  (School air raid shelter, now a museum, including air raids, and period
  shop.)
Eden Camp Modern History Theme Museum, Malton, North Yorkshire,
  YO17 6RT. Telephone: 01653 697777.
  (Ex-POW camp, now housing displays on many facets of the home
  front.)
The 1940s Experience, The Lincolnsfields Children's Centre, Bushey Hall
  Drive, Bushey, Herts. WD23 2ES. Telephone: 01923 233841.
  (1940s house, Dig for Victory garden, evacuee schoolroom – limited
  opening days.)
Geffrye Museum Trust, Kingsland Road, London, E2 8EA.
  Telephone: 020 7739 9893.
  (Excellent museum of period interiors.)
Home Front Experience, New Street, Llandudno, LL30 2YF.
  Telephone: 01492 871032.
  (Living history museum dealing with many facets of the home front.)
Imperial War Museum, Lambeth Road, London SE1 6HZ,
  Telephone: 020 7416 5320.
  (Many displays of home front items, plus temporary exhibitions and
  events.)
Imperial War Museum North, The Quays, Trafford Wharf Road, Trafford Park,
  Manchester M17 1TZ. Telephone: 0161 836 4000.
  (Many displays of home front items, plus temporary exhibitions and events.)
Land of Lost Content, The Market Hall, Market Street, Craven Arms,
  Shropshire SY7 9NW. Telephone: 01588 676 176.
  (An old-fashioned museum covering many facets of British home life in
  the twentieth century.)

Newhaven Fort, Fort Road, Newhaven, East Sussex, BN9 9DS.
Telephone: 01273 517622.
(Ex-defensive fort, now housing displays including facets of the home front.)

The Severn Valley Railway, The Railway Station, Bewdley, Worcestershire DY12 1BG. Telephone: 01299 403 816.

1940s Swansea Bay, Elba Crescent, Crymlyn Burrows, Swansea SA1 8QQ.
Telephone: 01792 458864.
(Displays include interiors, shops, bar and Anderson shelter.)

Stockport Air Raid Shelter, 61 Chestergate, Stockport, Cheshire, SK1 1NE.
Telephone: 0161 474 1940.
(An underground public shelter network with wardens' post, a first aid post and 16-seater toilets.)

Winston Churchill's Britain at War Experience, 64–66 Tooley Street, London Bridge, London SE1 2TF. Telephone: 020 7403 3171.
(A series of scenes and displays of various facets of the home front.)

There are also a number of annual or regular events including;

The Mid Hants Railway 'Watercress Line', The Railway Station, Alresford, Hampshire, England, SO24 9JG. Telephone: 01962 733810.
(Regular 1940s weekends)

The War and Peace Show, The Hop Farm, Beltring, Paddock Wood, Kent, TN12 6PY. Telephone: 01304 813945.
(Annual event bringing re-enactors from all over Europe and beyond.)

The 1940s Society, c/o 90 Lennard Road, Dunton Green, Sevenoaks, Kent, TN13 2UX. Telephone: 01732 452505.
(Regular meetings with speakers, film showings, etc Magazine with many 1940s events listed)

In addition there are frequently 1940s weekends at many museums, halls, houses and hotels, as well as 1940s dances, and a host of other events, which are usually great fun for the enthusiast and novice alike. Wearing period clothing is normally optional, whether immaculately researched, a nod in the right direction, or strictly modern.

INDEX